• • • • • • • • • • • • • • • • • • •

The Little
Seamstress

• • • • • • • • • • • • • • • • • •

•••••••••••••••••

The Little
Seamstress

•••••••••••••••••

Phil Hall

ACKNOWLEDGEMENTS
The publisher wishes to thank the Canada Council for the Arts and the Ontario Arts Council for their generous support of our publishing program.

Library and Archives Canada
Cataloguing in Publication

Hall, Phil
    The little seamstress / Phil Hall.

Poems.
ISBN 978-1-897141-32-8

    I. Title.

PS8565.A449L58 2010
C811'.54   C2009-907139-8

DESIGN
Zab Design & Typography, Toronto

EDITED FOR THE PRESS
by Erín Moure

COVER ARTWORK
Janieta Eyre, *The Book of Small Souls*

TYPEFACE
Clarendon

Printed in Canada

THE CANADA COUNCIL | LE CONSEIL DES ARTS
FOR THE ARTS | DU CANADA
SINCE 1957 | DEPUIS 1957

ONTARIO ARTS COUNCIL
CONSEIL DES ARTS DE L'ONTARIO

for Ann

L'éclair me dure.

René Char

Laity

O I'm in
the parade—I'm there
  with the pipers—but I'm playing a leaf-blower

there's ground-beef in the collector lanes

I miss Feliciano

Bravity

It is not you—it is the door—& then the phone
I open myself to cradle phonemes now that you are these things

......

You found my key
the melody-wound—now open me
suck my grief

plug in some amp
from fairyland—dampen my hand
you blew too few

......

Before you died
you tie-dyed—livid

a flux-nova—absurd worn now
but still vehement splattered twisting

an unrepentant old Trot
as if louder held sway

......

My real feet in my knees
I kneel—to go with you

Some Sieges

Here—interference by hay—suggests kinship
to seek a place—yields—to plant wire

the upkeep—you can't imagine—it's hopeless
blasted pine-meat—the yellow car alone

hence to go on repeating the supine of *to go*
to submit a neck of land

......

As I gather the phone's gist

I build an igloo of disposable diapers
soiled—then folded & tabbed—into white bricks

storm's here—I crawl inside
snow-blind / deaf—to sacrosanctities

(hide scraped by mouth-flicker)
pleasantries (gouges) / arrangements (wind-whistle)

blubber—to stop the holes—*vaster realms*
in this black spoon

......

She never dreamt old nails could get so angry

until she had backpacked in to rust-coloured headwaters
& heard Clawhammer's horns in heat

It is always crazy-making
(she wrote in her journal—in her tent—in the glacier's shadow)

to be beaten for your strength
& then not accepted as part of what you hold

......

Began
ended

up-ended
rent

rant-
-dented

I beg
an end

it pends

......

A hush is a constellation
snow settles in the intricacies of the bush

stars always have seemed to draw / aim / snip

but them elusive valences
it took an old mountain woman to see through

Ruth Stone invited 'em in—as viscera

while others heard pebbles hit thorns in tubes
& bragged *rain*

......

The old woman on the next farm
patched the knee of my pants

O it bends a root or gesture exquisite
to be born to drunks

while I stood there wearing them
a bitten thread—then she gave me an onion

O torture the spitting image in circles
half-trying to do any better

......

All fungi ears
the dead standing birch
keener each drizzle

a book-mould smell
devoured as geography & ticket

sails trimmed to steaming trunks
felled

a glare un-aims pardon

......

Their gables harvest moose

two scalloped bone-waves
deep in a tin sky

I ate smoked heart—to be polite
puked brown troughs & spikes

don't laugh—I had a vision

my mouth leaks water-lilies

I paint like Freud

Mask & Chore

To stage *The World*—cast the audience
reduce its role to one word—in English of course

rhubarb rhubarb rhubarb rhubarb rhubarb

so it sounds like the extras are talking to each other
 in the crowded streets & arenas—but they aren't

to get real—then—might mean to heckle reruns of *The World*
 through the frayed weave of an antique Alphabet Sampler

but who would choose that mask & chore
 over the part of Rhubarb behind the Stars?

......

As she crouches naked under sugar
the men hoot & clap & chant for her to breach

Beau-dy! Beau-dy! Beau-dy! Beau-dy!

the biggest thrill is screaming drunk together
 to see her burst out nude—is the excuse

the game sought most—is to not let on
 they dread her name so

......

  As the garter snake
swallows the leopard frog hind-first
 its eyes come down over its eyes
as if to make
             (& this is the worst)
 a mask for its meal as it cries

Blur

This fur merchant's child-bride
just drank gun powder

he will sail to France for another

she reigns under all we have read

......

Once ruptures
hoisting continents riddled with guilt

but *Upon* recites at bedtime
a protection-song very fast like *maresy doats*

weaving us into only sound vestments

......

This mask is old running shoes
where we went is how we look

a wild face has worn us home
from our jog by the river that is nothing

......

These binoculars
my handcuffs

Isolopia

Policing the clock
I try to make it walk a straight line

by pushing it like a lawnmower

its drunk-on-green blade
tears up the fine I write

......

Between the outhouse & the wedding bed
a little fist that parents both has rotted

when the prostate poem is finally finished
it is so stupid—too small—too late...

the time devoted to it—has not ratcheted rot

......

From clogged Loch Awe
back upstream until—a ship on a mountain!

a ship in a bottle on a mountain!

a ship in a baby bottle on a mountain!

nowhere to go—nothing to do

Carmen Jondo!

The good pen
is no good for this

I don't know what *this* is

but I know the pen I found in the road
 is the best way to find out
for me

 the good pen
I just like to hold

......

The fruit on the bone is an ocean

pick a word—*the pressure*—a boat!

......

 People are like pens
in pens—they lie around for years
 they never write anything

sometimes they dry up (so what)
 but mostly the ink is in there
dark & ready

 wolves in marbles
foxfire-hoof patents
 etiquette-muskies

Epyllia

r

 little pump
at pantry sink

 daddle-daddle
wood-rot bait

 come out
I drink am

 the well am
we

Folding-Fork

I don't bring my folding-fork on reading tours anymore

I can't take it on planes (it might be confiscated as a dangerous weapon)

It is dangerous because it solves for good a need

At home I often touch the initials scrimshawed into its bone handle

I hold a gift some man ate with for months at sea in the 1800s

And never think to use it myself for what it was made for

It has become a metaphor of the kind of poem that turns on itself to make
emptiness sing—the inwardness & ruthlessness of a line

I really am the kind of person who bites the loose skin between his thumb
& index finger when he's worried he might have sounded like a doofus

Airports began as heaven's basements—they have evolved into prison-malls

Scanned—no past gets past (unless cartooned)—& unique is eunuch

But hand-to-mouth—our first crude way of feeding each other—what Bakhtin
calls our *collective medieval folk body*—we hordes—waltz right through

Past the terror in Security's glittering eyes

Above Dawson

I wasn't what you'd call happy necessarily but I was out of bed dressed
& off looking for the cemeteries on the mountain above Dawson

I glanced back down—the whole City was there—just a village really—an
oil-can-roofed squat gussied by Parks Canada at the delta of those two
disgruntled wild rivers—the Yukon & the Klondike

An ice bridge—a blue-grey Museum/Court House—the yellow pressed-tin
Service bank—the "How to Build a Fire" hills insouciant & unscathed—
diamond-toothed from the fire towers

Majesty biding Time in clawed crevasses—numb—looked back at my
legendary pain & didn't so much as caw—but I had my big moment anyway

I saw my pain as a quaint stash of pornography from the 50s—nudist-
colony moms & pops with kids in buzz-cuts tossing inflated globes or
reading Albert Schweitzer together

All faded orange by now—perversely clean—but with blacked-in paper teeth
I suck on for sustenance & inquisition

There it was—not Dawson City—my Pain-City—*islanded in fog or sleep my
wet-nurse that old slut dog-dirty outmoded home from the trinket sea*

I was gone—writing in my head—*Will I never be full witness where I am?*

Then—behind or below the City—for an instant despite
myself—I saw (surviving in the north & the folks I'd met)
what tourists like me never find—& never stop trying to
find—without staying put

A dredged joy

Porn

My just-washed old hair loosening & lightening in the wind—I walk down our deadfall path to Otty Lake—my buckskin coat the only sun

Two partridges—wary—stepping beak-regal—pump rough & fluster up—thrown books fanning off into underbrush...

The rain has ruined the purple mushrooms—their black gill-feathers now a sticky guck

I am so gratefully dumb about "small lot management"

Our parents & the kids' pets buried or scattered here (along this lichened edge of Shield—from Georgian Bay to the Ottawa River)

I need socks—oat cakes—a hair-cut—bug-spray—but my mind is on some young woman who glances back over her shoulder—past her bare & open ass—with a look of fear & resignation—that should shame me—but excites me

As a boy I was opened & hurt—so I've always understood—if not shared—a flinch of her degradation...but part of me is also abuser—wants to...

Something—so I don't have to be her...

Instead I pray—*Conscience—Immune System—Earth's Atmosphere—Topsoil—the Periodic Table—bless us*

She could be my daughter—18 next month—the creature I love more than...

I'm 53—my Grey-Wing head bowed to mulch & kindling

When I walk back up the path to our log cabins—a doe is at
the salt-lick—tick-bitten—scratched tame

We will watch each other until guck turns regal

Windsor

They sure had it in for me—& my white bug—those little bastards

They pushed it down the alley—tore the gear shift out of the
floor—I had to use a screw-driver to change gears to get to my
orderly job on time (the old age home—Villa Maria—under the
Ambassador Bridge) on those cold mornings

Zany Steve Dahl—on the radio from Detroit—while the windows
defrosted—would be doing voices—Ali—Olive Oyl—between the
songs—that late 70s mishmash

Whip It! by Devo & coming up later *The Chicken Song* by Doug &
the Slugs

We were behind & above—a Laundromat—upstairs from Bron
Wallace—Ron Baxter—& little Jeremy in his *Thank You Dr Lamaze*
t-shirt—the four of us playing euchre Saturday nights

We were ancient history—or a new breed of citizens—even used
cloth diapers—until they all vanished from the Laundromat
dryer—I chased a grey van two blocks

They pushed my bug over—upside down—on its hood—in a pool
of its own gasoline—you could see the front axle was rusted right
through—the radio blaring—the wheels spinning—my landlord
screaming Italian at me

Then the bikers next door (who seemed decent) broke in
one grim weekend—stole my dad's little German 22 in its
case & all my records—I still miss *Blowin' Yr Mind* by Van
Morrison—it had "TB Sheets" on it

One of my final nights there—I had—Ani—her name was—
over—from behind—on the orange carpeted floor of our
living room—while my wife was at work at Mother's Pizza

(The waitresses had to wear these tan laced bodices & the
walls of the booths were decorated with antique photos—
nameless threshing crews)

My son was 2—the first *Star Wars* had just come out &
because his name is D'Arcy kids called him Darthy Vader

He could climb from his crib—had heard something—was
scared I guess

He was standing in the doorway—in a plastic diaper—
breathing sleep-gunk & watching us make the desperate
blind alien we were up to

He said—*Daddy?*

Settling In

The insects in Brazil were sitting pretty

I was getting married the next day—Jan had been hanging with
Billings (but no one had seen him for a few days)

We were on the patio at Yum-Yum's or Yo-Yo's—talking about her
graduate work on bug-screens—a special thread & weave—her own
design—an alternative to pesticides

Her tongue could butter lust with regret while adding just a bi-twist
of indifference

We were all such studious reprobates that summer as we began
the evasive processes of settling in without letting ourselves be
brought down

Screwing in-flight as we chose our graves—a PhD—marriage—the
Niagara River

For years I thought—*At least I'm not Billings*—who had seemed too
ambitious to read for fun—too formal to ever surprise paper with a
sandwich

As poets back then we all stank of childhood—kept forgetting
our lines & freezing into frescoes—then blurting any obscenity to
shock the plot along

These days *Wouldn't-Hurt-A-Fly* is my persona

Ylang

Of *me* parted by *us* I yodel *muse*

Inside your voice bees huddle honey behind a falls

Only I know where the hive is & why the cataracts smell of
buckwheat clover

Last night I dreamt that while I slept alone in the dark on
my back—uncovered—naked—with the fan on full-blast—my
short-hairs genuflecting to the winch of the snowstorm—you
kissed me—right where my pelvic bone juts for you to kiss it

When I woke up in the dream—your kiss had stayed as a
tattoo—a little pale blue sea-horse tattoo—your brand

When I woke up from the dream of waking up—it was
there—it was still there

When I touch it I hear the sea again—that sea that has no
name or planet as you & I have no name or planet

Bring me your pulse—I will put my oiled ear to your inner
thigh—where a Nile courses round the pelvic bone

Bring me your pulse for my pulse to push on—I will put my
open mouth to the throb above your collarbone—where the
Gulf Stream floods north surging your voice to its deltas

A stand-up desk in a bare room—a glistening hardwood
floor—open windows full of waves—in one corner for us
alone to fall on—a bed—a white one

A library in a turret room got to by a spiral stair—you returning
on our one bike—in taffeta & jeans—with peaches!

A swim together in the afternoon—a long slow intense siesta—red
snapper in a beach fire—dandelion greens we pick together

Your chewing-while-shrugging kiss—my ocean—wordlessness
holy—laughter holy

Variorum

White

  S becoming P
enacts a closure at its head
  gives up its river-spine
for the straight-edge

  doubt's old & crooked
but has intricate uses
  skepticism inefficient as a rose
we looked up / the dove flew

  Saul dead
in the road—wakes as Paul—glowing
  taking the pledge
under his mare

  indifferent she bends
away her turnpike neck

......

Omen

I see myself across a dark room

sitting on a blanket in an open doorway
the games were—*House / Lost / Sugarfoot / Gag*

the hero always the smart horse—another mouth
stands in shadow—walls / leaves raked into
lines—the dad gone or furious—the real ones lean

into glare smoking & laughing at
something I've done—the horse trying to warn by neighs
& snorts—that mom she just adored them
kids—his breath & hers churning in cyclones—adored

them only if they pretended to
sleep—a slap of light has separated me from
the pretence of being a body

way over here for this one omen only I
love my young real ones & their baby

how we all fought for a turn to be the horse who

wasn't playing

......

Dawn

 Let the hydro stay down
grope for edges in the weakening murk

 the frog that births tads out its mouth
thrives—& you are innocent

 of what your dreams half-lost
half-hint

Origin Of A Lullaby

Don't be discouraged by the prosaic origins of poems

Let the circus come to town—write it all out—the bearded flashbacks—the two-headed incriminations

Let the stories set up their Big Top—let the barkers carney the rubes

Behind the trailers a giraffe is giving birth

Far from the roots of doors—their hands relaxed claws—the trapeze family is snoring in harmony—what did you think the poem was— join them

If you are lucky—when you wake up—this tent city will be a field again—the circus will have pulled up & rolled away—your childhood will have joined it

The newborn giraffe is in your arms—the ungainly—squirmy— actual—creature

Sing to it—to help it stand for the first time—like an unfolding hinged ruler

In a memory of the creaking of ropes is the origin of a lullaby

Try again—devoid of guile or hoopla

Ulterior Thule

(stump)

 My archive
is not about me
 or itself
says the sun

*I dream of quietly passing under a fat black cross that has
too long blocked me from seeing the sun*

*But each time I step through the shadows of its outstretched
arms—a shrouded body on it falls upon me—is me—this
body—these my heavy curtains*

*Whose folds have been traced down to beaten paths nowhere
in centuries of paint autopsy pituitary-phosphorous*

*I dream the I has a bag of stories over its head & is
screaming!*

......

The smallest sounds have the biggest centres

One little goddess grill-cores old 45s

A cheap but crucial device—a trinket-maze bestirred—it
makes the big centres of the smallest sounds smaller—the
whirling around them hearably still

......

Even Pytheas of Massalia (325 BCE) presents us with a foggy half-aquatic burning muddy edge—interpretation of one element as another

The British Isles vanish or emerge again under application of magic

There is no longer any distinction—no actual mists over peat-bog— no land or sea or air—but a mixture of tarn *traeth* lungs eyes stumps tussocks

Where once was the *ilys* of *Thoule* or *Thyle*—now becomes a glassy expanse traversed neither wholly on foot nor by just boat

......

The details won't matter—them turncoats

The secrets won't matter—stolen purses gagging on branches

What might matter is the errors—that goof-ball!—can you believe they study the nervy quirks of his handwriting!

If error is character then she was a real cracked plate—somehow crawled up a stick & spun itself absurdly!

As record of error the notebooks sprawl—but what if the hand— poised between a fist & a shadow turkey—gets gussied as an icon to point to details & secrets?

......

We chart our course by such aromatic flawed victuals: *Down
The Dark Streets Alone* by Lilian Victoria Norden

A memoir of girlhood in the 1920s—her affair with Frederick
Horsman Varley (self published—unedited—Vancouver 1982).

The grease of the creature becomes graph-pikes & replicas—
design

......

The cut-out tongues of these Cretan boots make good pot-
holders

Or perhaps it helps to remember Rimbaud's comment about
Lamartine: *still there are too many seers strangling in old
forms*

Or get all mushy over Schubert's *lieder* without understanding
a word

......

It was later than metaphor when the arts jury finally finished

Our brains smudged thumbprints on windows in barns at dusk

They gathered into loops the press release they had written together

Failed lariat throw—no—no—cartoon speech-bubble lassoing grass

They wished words well everywhere—effusively—because of the hour

Goodnight conjunctions—you cute little buggers

They were laughing but they were sick of each other

Night like velvet—bolts of it in bins—night a tsunami of pepper

......

To brier the pulse then—a shared asunderwaking—each line a quill
stitched below the skin between the words

An ardent appeal to the hearth-god Compulsion: *snap-snap us in
Your unpredictable buck-&-wing*

How far out of themselves our vibrant partial truths have been lured

Yet the ensemble swears its intent never prose

......

The midwife's broken the water—doctor's on her way

Rest your head—little father—on your arms on the table—&
dream about a small boy whose soft-spot won't harden

In a doll hobby store the dad buys little skylights—half-
bubbles of hard plastic—to tape over the boy's soft-spot
under his ball cap

One night the dad peeks in at the son asleep & there's this
blue film projecting from the boy's soft-spot onto the wall...
*quick vanilla monstrosities—fathom goop—juggled panic—
fries—Vikings bartering trolls for quahogs—a hoola-dancer
in a jar with a few marbles...*

Wake up—bearded! Where are your glasses?

A toddler is untying your laces

There's a note

......

Where they used to keep the lions or monkeys—they now
keep gardening equipment

This park & petting-farm is as far from their birth
townships as some folks ever got or get

We are still only two hours from where nothing ever changes

(The old boys' network is just one normal sentence after
another)

Gawk in through bars at the tools—their still blades jammed
with almost-edible encyclopedic dirt

The blizzard-bird-of-cultivation—in captivity

......

From the clutter & confusion of shared days—all the usual
doubt worry disappointment hope—somehow it gets written

Old before dry—other wise—long-stewed—ungenerous to
memorizers—a grope crevassing rhymes—flirting with its
own inattention

It goes—well no one quite knows where it goes when it's read

It is a useless but needed invention

It makes our dead less dead

......

Oh sure some still hope to have less to do with memory
& sentiment the further our expedition paddles into the
element-confusion of the ulterior—but look—along the far
horizon-edge—New Sentences rear their grated feudalisms

......

What topsoil tells the hand—the hand tells a pencil—a pencil
tells type—type tells a program—a program tells brains—
brains tell the gods—& the gods tell topsoil...

Feed the pinch or the swell!

......

*I can't flail my way through these sinuous tatterplush
vaudeville burgundies*

*So half-awake I pound my arms to try to part my fizzing
muscles & slip through into the blinding welcome cells
reserve*

Not for the pin-cushion gods—but for the Fool

Backwater

g

 The abominable
is a mountain of shredded paper

 blizzard memo pom-pom

yet I love a *g* like a squashed *o*
 with a dribbled reflection-tail

& a little wave sipping its brow

Doodle

#?! pen won't write—so scratch
blank wave swoops—nib-dent maelstrom

& slowly—a leak—nightjar-flux

ego—egg-bone—be gone—ack—oot
to quill-writ ink-rigging—to tongue-split fathom-fount

each keel-tilt a wing-flap
once underway—then what—a book

but the sea—flag snap—raw plot scraps
the thread of the Tampax coming out of you Ariadne

in Voice's lab I rinse a crock of dialed ears
trough wallop *fathom-farm*

circle in circle out
from mere ache—to miracle

(oracle)
form

Sawmill Tuning

In the pines there are birds

my darkness isolation-cell
  endless river black thread

fat pipe on sea bottom in grey crud
  concourse of ink in pens all pens a canal
system of locks between talks / one swung

  bridge / at the cheap spout of each beak
at the Tamil protest the cop said
  your ear is bleeding / in my back pocket
a Black Panthers business card

  "the critical chain across the critical path"
(asleep / a knock / a leap / Porlock)
  the chorus of water / the water-chorus

the personal only looks personal
  my darkness a banal scrawk

the golden bird the passenger

Backwater

A woman takes off her bombshell
& puts on her chicken—takes off her chicken
& puts on her bombshell—non-stop

as a man's swagger sags
to unveil his mother as an old man
in suspenders & mustachios

in a Booth Tarkington farce
at a local theatre when he was a boy
& didn't recognize his own mother

then did—halfway through
& had to be taken out—screaming
or are we talking two women here

or are we talking two men
either way silent a baby grand
in a shut-down woollen mill—high-strung

above a waterfall
at midnight—a waterfall
an infidel in a crinoline

Reaney

Little Olson—that drunken blowhard
really laid it down solid a time or two—kingfishers & satyr-bikers
 flung from a prolonged—sloppy—*Timber!*

meanwhile—our local giant
 his marionettes enacting the Orange wars

his happy chicken harnessed to a carriage
 & all three rings of his barn circus spinning windfall spokes
unbeknownst in of all places London Ontario

 where Whitman came to discuss cosmic consciousness
with Richard Maurice Bucke MD—where Greg Curnoe rode his paintings

 on glass around town—where journaling Roy McDonald abides...
Olson & Whitman—the Push & the Yawp—amount to not much around here
 but when that big red heart of his let loose for the open highlands

our school-bell townships—amalgamated—went digital
 the killdeer's eggs lost a protector

& the Nihilist Spasm Band pulverized *God Save The Queen*

A Ripple

At the fire tower on the Second Dome
above Dawson at bright midnight solstice
 (the Yukon widening around Tr'ondëk islands)

mosquitoed cursive—eating rhubarb pie
 at the top edge of the guide-bookish
over into the uneven eventless mouth mine

 Bill the shy fire ranger plays *Scotland the Brave*
half-bore as best he is able on old reeds
 his breath—fog plumbing bagpipes—a ripple

of the Periodic Table (our ground-sheet / flag)
 as the drone & the lilt in the stop-cocks try
to skin this flung church of its glare...

 Mom never could tolerate the pipers swinging
their big hairy volcanoes on the 4th of July
 without crying—for lost reasons...

may pulse widen until blood means nothing
 glint gape trickle hoof mud...

Lucy Locket

Dot matriculated—had us—died young
the little she told—the bits I remember—legend

 the flat stones in that wall were brought by barge from England
a ride on a swimming buffalo—the bull—Napoleon—what a loud snorter

 lightning boils corsets / flasks—knocked Erma the length of the pantry
& God's brogue to the just-dead—*Gy home yr wee ones need ye*

 Lucy Locket by herself in the lighthouse in the storm
she has to try to light the big light—for me—the captain—of a toothpick

 I steer toward the one story that flares inside many half-truths
though I know now that her light on shore is fear

......

 Bee Farm married Beef Arm—The Tickler married The Stickler
(& the wrong red sentence ends in common-law with sustenance)

Revenge

In one story I made up that year
a deprived killer groomed then tortured the inept
(who were "the new innocent")

for throwing away their album covers!
(each scratched record stood bare & separate
in the whisk of its slot—wide-eyed

near the arms of an old divan
that had been ridden to slick black
by 8 no 9 dim kids)

my glass gravel-pit cathedral was already underway
even back then (its bright canyon spiring deep into scarpland
its purple vaunts leaded against operose earth)

on muddy grass (in my last darned socks)
I hovered—supervising—all rim

Prodigal

My slobbered song
this incarcerated step...

always knew (in my denial)
I'd come back to this swing-bridge

to these shut locks—this deep volume
of both lakes between castle doors

to these clanging chevron gangways
above each slimed gate

to this matt-wobble of self leaning out-over...

have spoken how a spoke speaks
a many-whirred one from hub to rim

am the wound the treble clef smells of
(my say bluffing *of* after sorry *of*)

between praise & forgiveness
between Pidgeon Lake & Sturgeon Lake

this water-book / arrow-cask
measures an allotment of ink

I am now drunk by
opened unto...

Stephen Foster

OK
is a corral—*I have heard that said*

& Miserable is a mighty river
we each have a secret name for
 but never use until we are in it

alone again (twang)
 one rubber boot sucked off in the mud
& lost forever—though *forever* wears pretty
 thin...

so you're fording the mighty Mis
 & an overhead on the overpass—a live wire
(snapped by a gravel truck with its empty bucket up)
 comes whipping too fast to see
down along the shore

 without thinking
you go under where Fort Knox thunder
 is a wide illegal pipe dumping crap
right into that pastoral song got made up

 one time—lickity-split
on a dare & a swig—*as we all sup sorrow*
 with the poor

gonna take *how am I* out & shoot it
 you come too

To Listen

To listen—they lean forward—kids do
when you read to them—they *list*
 they know how to listen

but adults think of things they have to do
 they lean back—tick off items on a list
while you read—it's to themselves they listen

 kids pull the fire out of a word
drawing its heat up into themselves
 by magic—like a cheroot above an oil lamp used to

but adults have been burnt by words
 they know what not to do—have trained themselves
to pulse like neon—don't waver the ways they used to

 if you have a choice—read to kids
without a school board close at hand
 to tick off which words have been outlawed

lean in to kids
 read a monstrosity like a fire in the hand
a classic that was once outlawed

Our Miserable Life
by William Steig

She who absorbs both papers—I try sarcastic
how did you manage to get that bath-robe so filthy
she is writing to-do notes on her hand
& snickers at me—indulgently

I who find elastics wherever she goes
looking for that good pen of hers once more
she accuses me of tidying it away somewhere
(I did but can't remember where now)

she who once hiked to the base-camp at Mt Everest
I who poisoned the dogs with hot dogs in Withrow Park
as we wistfully toboggan the duties
hammock the sulks

The Alphabet

I tried to be that funny friend
who always has something interesting to say
 & makes a lot of sense—but is also a bit of a wing-nut

my poems had my friends in them
 so they'd recognize themselves—where we were—what we did
oh I'd take them somewhere else too

 not far enough to scare them—just outside the firelight
into the long grass—then back—but now I only have 26 friends
 I give a damn about in a poem

I am Godard's *Weekend*—which I haven't seen but I hear is
 full of ruthless accidents among friends
(this tort-costume doesn't come off)

 I am the n of a broken h
I am half a friend—an end

The Brunt

To be white
helps & silent
 & a little fucker

in the white field a monster—silence

 its nose—a cursor-pulse

Filigree

Split maple / a Red Bird match alights in
gup guff hum flummery

this roar / oar / ar / r's inner platelets & folio-shades

these creature-cells the Ojibwa disport throb-wild
ash scroll-white in patches / *safety pattern is*

my innards not slime-on-vellum—but a ritual textured glow

shaggy-mane & raven / the log breaks / the stove ticks
not to understand / but return / elsewhere

......

So stupid & still am

couldn't hear speed or silence
thought silence a sculpture in a park

speed all dong & séance

let a sculpture be a fallen totem / theatre train
(bears' heads fluttering under the waves of an inlet)

off-kilter / let song / & dance / usher in / alert calm

on one leg I try to bow but my goat mask falls off
as I trip over it—my prayer comes out—*duh*

to read & wait—open & hum

my great story / migratory

The Little Seamstress

Breath—done to death—is our is

all us singers sewing the clipper

 afraid of writing / afraid of not writing
failure ugly mug rage mewling looted well

 raiding gruesome oaths opens I's double doors
in a splayed notebook an apostrophe hovers

 broken pencil tip tongue flame flick
go stand on a chair beside an ear—*hear*
 or climb a ladder—one rung—*Hear*

see *Hall* as a laugh by the tracks
 home as an empty chair—a hole—& me
normal day—am in it normal too—but as if in a

 too—but as if in a / too—but as if in a / car wash
her decks scrubbed raw with *holystone* & sea foam
 the poem wants broken through to textures below

how might an all-ogist of periods widen netherly?
 chunks of English gravestone plunged in buckets of curl

hauléd up overside—for slop of planks bright-wilde
 (from *I'm beautiful* to *imbue* / from *maré* to *mere*)

destination: dense lurch-weave

 Anacoluthon

The Brunt

Swim alone panic drown

tongue-creature in mouth-cave grunting *unh-unh*
 the beast with two paperbacks

North South East West / Birth Prison Hospital Death
 of being mediocre arrogant cowardly small-spirited provincial
of becoming the bath-water to dry up a *no* a hole

 haven't written never will can't read write a gurgle
sex to heal the sacred where the altar was desecrated
 each person a cave the other finds & hides in
confines & confides in no light beast-wallow

 till the Os are barned hungry-full
till the ease-quilts lift shook raucous
 till the beak & the stubble-droplet
till the chevron's labour & the under-claw
 till the lowing of the swung bell's

depth-charge sleep
 address corrupted / reception muted
to draw the I across the O
 now that TV has numbed the abscess of the Folk Tale
this hesitant beseech as powers caution us

 against unison "for health or religious reasons"
sex one of the last wild parklands
 pornography logs it illness pollutes it
romance lies about it marriage vacations there

a self-sufficient anti-social joy-torsion
I's stretching each other to O's
 poetry hitching into the mudnight sin

water in a skeleton-costume dances
 to swim like a frog with a stone in its mouth

dear treader

Alderliefest

I take my thumb out of my mouth & hold it high

have sucked so long & hard—*two* nails are growing from one
with a split down the middle of both—old dream-plug

the barn has big tin balls on spikes / the house—skewers

my tree-fort lunging at sea has only this fruit-rod

......

In the mailbox lobby of the post office beside the park
in Bobcaygeon night-long studying the lights on the bridge

pink or green—the bugs on the window of the barber shop
little outhouse sailboats tacking identically reflections

the acid wearing off in tail-snap-sighs insincere
& crackled chemitecture whaa-whaas

......

Something just un-happened so thin I fit in it

An Apprenticeship Ends

Neruda's or my green-glass demon-trinkets
balanced on clear planks in porthole windows

(their flaw-seeds curated vanishing-acts)

our Bristol blue depression-ware kraken-toys
 nodding off on watch in ivy windows facing the sea

......

 I hug his giant promotional shoe
 it's a corset coffin—a larynx wheelchair

his Parral tanner's dummy-horse

is the buffalo my mother rode as it swam
 that I made up—sue me—we are afraid

......

 Of the sea—for one—it is inimitably unclear
& doesn't give a—though we lust after

 its Shakespearean rent-asunder disguises anyway

& anything—including us—can be the sea
 wearing our little captain's suits

......

Waving—drinking / thinking / sinking—as one
this is work—real—vital—of mass—of struggle

nope—malarkey—enough—here goes

an open blind private dive
into lilting shanty-jaws—murk

L'Anti-Tête

The young mare growing head-first in the field

her abyss-fierce star-fruit / pumping buttressed torso gleam

all those full harbours under full-sail grunt-work

unfurled story-scrolls panicking in air—the sheer weight

of all that isn't—believed—the numbers alone enough to bend her

tulips & fronds to earth again fallow in the drizzle all morning

never lifting her muzzle's delicate rootlet-hairs

from the *of of of*

best known as grass

......

The plane trees were wearing their patchwork shadows
one eye-witness was reading a book

a novel / their mottled trunks

another report says—to step into such detail—to enter

a pause of light / clean-cut harmony / print-smudged canals

impossible / flame / flame of / of...

to become the same substance as the agent-char
now aggrandizingly blotting out

screen / beam / hood / elbow / squint...

reading engulfed yet unburnt

tree shadows painted on whitish stuccoed walls

along Sunday avenues nowhere 1910

......

After all the melodic ruthless couplings

of any one thing to any other by little *of*

soliloquy of rhubarb / fetlock of devil's paint-brush

there are still poets who profess to care

whether I have one ear

or two cars

Tinguely

Or stand on one leg
in a field of carriage parts

blacksmith rows
for auction tomorrow—at dusk a crop
of long spoke shadows
pulling in

pulling out
I am too many folk toys
amateur local gleaned tracts
S-shaped wrenches for Model-A Fords
stove-lid lifters with coiled handles...

to read any
of us as a solo—I—we—why

want my tiny word-machines to
falter burn & self-destruct
like Jean Tinguely sculpture-devices—wonky
enough to deserve to be treated as if
they are alive
& dying

& crying & lying
(I tried to plain-say my brains
out—with trees—not run a gauntlet
of Roman goddess knock-offs—the milk
I spilled on the Mona Lisa
dried clear)

I would call
 what we make back
from a proscenium or cameo

 slip loose the survey-halter

let imbalance
 share some cold black grass

Ululae

```
  an t
ry in g
 to bur rO
wu nd erm
 yr in g
```

Family famished pectin & rye

family famished pectin & rye

old book smell—a place gone still
where is he

in a forest they do not infest

on an island as pure as an o

......

Rake winter leaf-mulch off violets

am a small human small writer
large animal fountain-clawed

darkening a story above water

this mome nt tha tone th ism omen tt h at on
ethi smo men tt hat o net hi smo mento us is

full moon above birch
in daylight a dot at the end of a line

fu moo ove irch
ni ayli a do at e en do fal i

a stone-throw composing
hairy little green saids

......

As I light the fire
I hear the train

who if not you gone long

& rain

yet written
yet writ

......

Having left the city

my children grown
that maelstrom theirs—that mosh-pit

my maelstrom the coiled / barbed / gummed tongue
of the Polyphemus Moth butting its blue fur head on the glass
when I'm up late tungstening

reading Joseph Wood Krutch on deserts
or telling the moth where to get off my children
my reasons for even trying once
leaping dazed at the core of the big smoke

my drunkalogs metamorphosed
are talking fish who warn that stillness is not cowardice
nor prayer nor hope—just some other song & dance

as I sit on the stone I throw
at myself into the lake

yes bites me

......

I hear them—the cracks
as I fall through

unsure / doubting myself

these spaces between
 one winning definition & another...

 muddle's my route

 its tongue—this grope
whoosh

 from said
to be

......

 Witness the soft road
bum light from smoke & smoke from light

 I wish I had a spirit-food to suck at me like that

nothing sucks at me
 it sucks my boots right off my head while I'm sleeping
cuts their tongues out & boils them

 like a—like a bishop forgiving snow its trespasses

hey perfectly good tracks of mine
 have been shoved down sump-holes—deep
with a stick—by nothing

 until the stick too vanishes—& it no twig
I'm just saying...

......

Oh sure craft
texterity honed to an x

 no name or aim just focus

an ear for nothing
 or nothin

or g

......

Ph

 I with swollen head
behind empty chair

 See One Giant Piano Hammer!
(Tiniest Show Flops!)

 What-For sinks key
Who-For sits

......

To rename myself
the way the Hanshan-poet did
he became Cold Mountain
I'd be Otty Lake

Audie Murphy / Linda Lake
(early hero / old girlfriend)
last I saw her—I saw clear through her—really
a restless soul—the shallows stink

& the depths choke with weeds
but the sun on the surface—patient its light
before us & after us—*delight / two syllables*
delight / OK—try it now yourself

who equals where
nearly

......

My mud-puddle-lantern billows & glares
as it guides me to be shall-water without a splash

to be hark-earth—not to market—not a hoe

......

I'll stop writing
when my two herons cross the marsh at dusk

a paddle-boat is a thirsty dog

these are *letters*—as in *go ahead*—*spit it out*

the bob is back!

canopy / can of peas / *pli selon pli*

silent dark unfolded rulers gliding
crude—their shadows lapping lily pads

I accept my failures
but I do not accept my death

......

An acetylene pain
while tinkering

a stab that eats the stab
of focus like lime eats fishiness

a line widening to wall-wave-night
prow row ow o

my vast holdings...

lint on a nib

Acknowledgements & Notes

this moment that one this moment that one

• • • • • •

Thanks to the following publications & presses where parts of this book first appeared: *Forget, The Walrus, Matrix, Brick, Jacket, Fiddlehead, Common Magic, poetics.ca*, above/ground, Running The Goat.

I am especially grateful to Mark Goldstein & Jay MillAr for the sustaining small press works they devoted to a couple of the poems included here: 'Variorum'—in *Ghost Gum* (Beautiful Outlaw) & 'Tinguely'—a broadside (BookThug).

Some folks &/or their works have been especially helpful: Tristan Tzara, Rae Armantrout, Robert Duncan, Andrew Vaisius, Nicky Drumbolis.

Thanks to Erín Moure for the acute generosity of her editing.

Thanks to The Berton House in Dawson City, Yukon, where I began some of these during a residency in 2006.

Thanks also to: the Griffin Poetry Prize, Test Reading Series, the Atwater Poetry Project & the Canada Council.

Thanks, Maureen, for the Ronald Johnson & Lorine Niedecker books—& thanks, Peter, for the Gibson tenor banjo!

Thule / Rosemary tells me (& she should know) / is pronounced *Too-lay*—but I still prefer to rhyme it with *fool*.

• • • • • •

"you come too"—Robert Frost

"asleep / a knock / a leap / Porlock"—the legend behind Samuel Taylor Coleridge's "Kubla Khan" (in a nut-shell)

"*The Little Seamstress*"—a print by Ian Hamilton Findlay / Richard DeMarco

Alington, A.F. *Some Sieges*. (Oxford: Basil Blackwell, 1964)

Steig, William. *Our Miserable Life*. (New York: Noonday, 1990)

......

Stephen Foster (1826—1864)

Lucian Freud (1922—

James Reaney (1921—2008)

Ruth Stone (1915—

Jean Tinguely (1925—1991)

......

Notley, Alice. *In the Pines*. (London: Penguin, 2007)

Taggart, John. *There Are Birds*. (Chigaco: Flood Editions, 2008)

Adamson, Robert. *The Golden Bird*. (Melbourne: Black Inc, 2008)

Duggan, Lorie. *The Passenger*. (St. Lucia: University of Queensland Press, 2006)

......

this moment that one this momentous is

PHIL HALL has taught writing & literature at the
Kootenay School of Writing, York University, Ryerson
Polytechnical University & many colleges. He has
been poet-in-residence at the University of Western
Ontario, the Sage Hill Writing Experience (SK), The
Berton House in Dawson City, Yukon, & elsewhere.
Trouble Sleeping (2000) was nominated for the
Governor General's Award for Poetry. *An Oak Hunch*
(2005) was nominated for the Griffin Poetry Prize in
2006. Hall lives near Perth, Ontario.